All recipes are tried and tested.
If you have any queries:

E-mail: nitamehta@email.com
Website: http://www.nitamehta.com

Nita Mehta's
MICROWAVE cookery

Nita Mehta

B.Sc. (Home Science), M.Sc. (Food and Nutrition), Gold Medalist

co-author
Tanya Mehta

SNAB
Publishers Pvt Ltd

Nita Mehta's
MICROWAVE
cookery

© Copyright 2002-2003 **SNAB** Publishers Pvt Ltd

WORLD RIGHTS RESERVED. The contents—all recipes, photographs and drawings are original and copyrighted. No portion of this book shall be reproduced, stored in a retrieval system or transmitted by any means, electronic, mechanical, photocopying, recording or otherwise, without the written permission of the publishers.

While every precaution is taken in the preparation of this book, the publisher and the author assume no responsibility for errors or omissions. Neither is any liability assumed for damages resulting from the use of information contained herein.

TRADEMARKS ACKNOWLEDGED. Trademarks used, if any, are acknowledged as trademarks of their respective owners. These are used as reference only and no trademark infringement is intended upon.

Reprint 2003
ISBN 81-7869-016-0

Food Styling and Photography: **SNAB**

Layout and laser typesetting :

National Information Technology Academy
3A/3, Asaf Ali Road
New Delhi-110002
☎ 23252948

Published by :

SNAB
Publishers Pvt. Ltd.
3A/3 Asaf Ali Road,
New Delhi - 110002
Tel: 23252948, 23250091
Telefax: 91-11-23250091

Editorial and Marketing office:
E-348, Greater Kailash-II, N.Delhi-48
Fax: 91-11-26235218 *Tel:* 91-11-26214011, 26238727
E-Mail: nitamehta@email.com
snab@snabindia.com
Website: http://www.nitamehta.com
Website: http://www.snabindia.com

Distributed by :

THE VARIETY BOOK DEPOT
A.V.G. Bhavan, M 3 Con Circus,
New Delhi - 110 001
Tel : 23417175, 23412567; Fax : 23415335

Printed by :

THOMSON PRESS (INDIA) LIMITED

Rs. 89/-

INTRODUCTION

Say good-bye to long hours in the kitchen. With the help of your microwave, prepare great tasting recipes in the shortest possible time.

Microwave leaves most foods tastier, retains their natural and fresh colour of food and there is no danger of food sticking to the bottom of your pan and getting burnt.

You can cook with very little oil. Cook, reheat and serve in the same dish and therefore, there is less washing up to do.

However, microwave cooking is a little different from conventional cooking. This book will help you actually cook the food in a microwave and get your money's worth.

I am sure you will enjoy using this book.

       Happy Microwaving!!   *Nita Mehta*

Contents

Introduction 5
Tips 9
About Microwaving Foods 10
Interesting Uses of Microwave 12

Indian 13

VEGETARIAN

Achaari Mushroom & Capsicum 14
Karele Lajawaab 18
Mughlai Vegetable Curry 24
Paneer Hara Pyaz 28
Kadhai Paneer 31
Khoya Matar 32
Mixed Masala Subzi 36

NON-VEGETARIAN

Murg Jalfrezi 16
Murg Jafrani 21
Tandoori Chicken 22
Shahi Machhi Patiala 26
Murg Haryali 34
Chicken Pulao 38
Kadhai Chicken 42

Spinach & Corn Pullao 40
Matar waale Chaawal 44
Khatte Mithe Baingan 45
Dal Maharani 49

Prawn Malai Curry 46
Chicken & Paneer Shashlik 50

CONTINENTAL, CHINESE & THAI 53

VEGETARIAN
Macaroni Cheese 60
Penne & Rice Baked in Spinach Sauce 62
Hungarian Paneer 64
Stuffed Tomatoes 72

NON-VEGETARIAN
Fish in Herb Sauce 54
Garlic Chicken 56
Chicken a' la Kiev 58
Chicken Stroganoff 67
Chicken with Mushrooms & Baby Corn 68
Chicken Hong Kong 70
Thai Green Chicken Curry 74
Chilli Chicken 77

Snacks 78

VEGETARIAN
Potato Based Pizza 81
Khandavi 83
Rawa Idli 88
Paneer & Grape Sticks 92

NON-VEGETARIAN
Tandoori Fish 79
Murg Malai Kababs 86
Chicken Tikka Tandoori 90

Desserts 94

Gajar Ka Halwa 95
Peaches in Sauce 96

Chocolate Walnut Cake 98
Lychee Pearls in Shahi Kheer 100
Vanilla Cake 102

Tips

- Do not microwave gravies & milk based food in shallow utensils. These may spill over.
- Do not pile food on top of each other. It cooks evenly & quickly when spaced apart.
- Avoid using square/rectangular bowls for cooking as the food gets overcooked at the corners.
- It is advisable to use ring shaped (round) shallow bowls with straight sides for speedy and even cooking.
- Do not add salt at the time of starting the cooking as it leads to increase in the cooking time.
- Food with its own moisture cooks faster. Addition of water increases the cooking time.
- Cakes may appear a little moist and undone after being microwaved for the specific time. Give it 5-10 minutes of standing time. A perfect cake will be ready.

About Microwaving Foods

Timings : If the timings are not set carefully, foods can become hard and leathery. It is always better to undercook than to overcook in a microwave. The larger the volume of food there is, the more timing is needed to cook it. 4 potatoes cook in 6 minutes, whereas 8 potatoes cook in about 9 minutes. Therefore, if the quality in a recipe is changed, an adjustment in timing is necessary. When doubling a recipe, increase the cooking time 50% approximately & when cutting a recipe in half, reduce time by about 40%.

Standing time : Food continues to cook for sometime, even after it is removed from the microwave. For example, the cake cooked in a microwave looks very moist and undone when removed from the oven after the microwaving, but after it is left aside for 8-10 minutes, it turns perfect.

Covering : Covers are used to trap steam, prevent dehydration, speed cooking time and help food retain its natural moisture. When covering with paper napkins, a good microwave coking practice, be sure to use a big one which will enable you to tuck the paper under the bottom of the cooking dish. Otherwise, it will tend to rise off the dish due to the air movement. A handy idea to keep in mind : a heatproof plate is a good substitute for a lid.

Stirring : If necessary, stir from the outside to the center because the outside area heats faster than the center when microwaves are in use. Stirring blends the flavours and promotes even heating. Stir only as directed in the recipes, constant stirring is never required, frequent stirring is rare.

Arrangement : The microwaves always penetrate the outer portion of food first, so food should be arranged with the thicker areas near the edge of the dish and the thinner portions near the center. Food such as tomatoes, potatoes and corn should be arranged in a circle, rather than in rows.

Sensitive ingredients : Ingredients like cheese, eggs, cream, condensed milk, mayonnaise etc., attract Microwave energy and so cook very quickly. Thus these can overcook causing them to toughen, separate or curdle. Use lower power settings to prevent this. It is the same principle as reducing the heat on a gas or electric burner.

INTERESTING USES OF MICROWAVE

- Making ghee. Keep the collected malai (milk topping) in a deep glass bowl and microwave to get desi ghee without burning your kadhai.
- Blanching almonds to remove skin.
- Freshening stale chips, biscuits or cornflakes. Place the chips or biscuits in a napkin, uncovered, for about 1 minute per bowl or until they feel warm. Wait for a few minutes to allow cooling and serve.
- Boiling (actually microwaving) potatoes. Wash potatoes and put them in a polythene bag. Microwave high for 5 minutes for 4 medium potatoes.
- Making khatti mithi chutney. Mix 1 tbsp amchur, 2 tbsp sugar, some water along with spices in a glass bowl. Microwave, stirring in between.
- Warming baby's milk bottle. Do check the temperature of the milk on you inner wrist. The bottle will not become hot, while the milk will.
- Softening too-hard ice cream, cream, cheese, and butter.
- Drying fresh bread crumbs, drying herbs.
- Melting chocolate, butter, jam, honey, etc. Dissolving gelatine.
- Sterilizing jars for storing home made jams and pickles.

INDIAN

Achaari Mushroom & Capsicum

Serves 4

7-8" ROUND, 1-2 " HIGH DISH

200 gms (1 packet) fresh mushrooms - cut into 4 pieces
2 capsicums - chopped into ¼" pieces
2 onions - cut into rings & separated
1 tsp dhania powder
1" piece ginger - cut into match sticks
2 tbsp oil
½ tsp each - saunf, jeera, rai and kalaunji
¼ tsp haldi, ¼ tsp amchoor
½ tsp garam masala, ½ tsp red chilli powder
1 tsp salt
1½ tbsp lemon juice, or to taste

1. In a dish micro high oil for 2 minutes.
2. Add saunf, jeera, rai & kalaunji to hot oil. Mix. Micro high for 1 minute.
3. Add onions and dhania powder. Mix well and micro high for 2 minutes.
4. Add haldi, amchoor, garam masala and red chilli powder. Mix well. Micro high for 1 minute.
5. Add ginger, mushrooms, salt and lemon juice. Mix very well.
6. Micro high for 8 minutes. Stir once in-between.
7. Add capsicum and mix. Micro high for 3 minutes and serve.

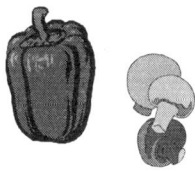

Murg Jalfrezi

Picture on cover　　　　　*Serves 4-5*

9" ROUND, 3" DEEP DISH WITH COVER

1 chicken (1 kg) - cut into 12 pieces
5 tbsp oil
1 medium onion
2-3 flakes garlic
4 tomatoes
2½" piece ginger
1½ tsp salt
1 tsp garam masala
1 tsp jeera (cumin) powder
1 tsp red chilli powder
¾ tsp haldi
½ tsp pepper (optional)
2 capsicums - cut into strips
½ cup cream or malai

1. Grind together onion and garlic to a paste.
2. Puree tomatoes and ginger together in a mixer.
3. In the dish, add oil, onion- garlic paste and haldi. Micro high uncovered for 3 minutes.
4. Add chicken. Add all other ingredients (pureed tomatoes and all the spices) except cream.
5. Mix well. Micro high covered for 10-12 minutes or till done.
6. Add cream and capsicum. Mix. Micro high covered for 3 minutes.
7. Let it stand for 2 minutes. Mix well. Garnish with chopped coriander leaves and garam masala. Serve hot.

Note: For less gravy, reduce tomatoes to 2½ tomatoes.

Karele Lajawaab

Picture on facing page   *Serves 4-5*

7-8 " ROUND, 1-2" HIGH DISH (FLAT DISH)

½ kg karelas (bitter gourd) - peeled, slit, seeds removed & rubbed with 1 tsp salt & 2 tbsp vinegar and kept aside for 2-3 hours

STUFFING

3 onions - chopped finely, ½" piece ginger - chopped finely
2 tbsp oil
1½ tsp moti saunf (big aniseeds)
¼ tsp haldi, ½ tsp salt, 3/4 tsp amchoor (dried mango powder)
½ tsp red chilli powder, ½ tsp garam masala, 3/4 tsp dhania powder

YOGURT COATING

½ cup thick curd - hung in a muslin cloth for 15-20 minutes
1½" piece ginger - crushed to a rough paste
¼ tsp salt, ½ tsp red chilli powder, ¼ tsp garam masala

1. Peel karelas. Give a cut in the centre lengthways. Carefully remove all the seeds. Sprinkle salt and vinegar and rub inside and over the karelas. Keep aside for 2-3 hours or more. You could do this part of the work in the morning and put away the karelas in the fridge, if they have to be prepared for dinner.
2. Wash karelas well to remove bitterness. Rub some oil on them. Micro high covered for 8 minutes on a plate or a flat dish.
3. In a flat dish, micro high 2 tbsp oil for 3 minutes.
4. Add saunf. Mix well. Add onions and ginger. Sprinkle haldi, salt, dhania, red chilli powder and garam masala Mix very well. Micro high for 7 minutes. Stir once in between.
5. Fill the stuffing in the karelas. Keep aside.
6. Mix curd with ginger paste, salt, red chilli and garam masala. Keep aside.
7. Arrange all the karelas in the dish, side by side. Put half the curd on them and spread to cover all the karelas. Turn the karelas and put the left over curd on them. Spread to cover well. Keep aside.
8. At the time of serving, micro high for 3 minutes and serve immediately.

Murg Jafrani

Serves 4-5

9" ROUND DISH, 3" DEEP

1 chicken (800-900 gms) - cut into 8 pieces
2 tbsp lemon juice
½ cup cream, ½ cup curd (made from full fat milk)
1 tsp salt, 1 tsp garam masala, 1 tsp dhania powder, 1 tej patta (bay leaf)
chopped fresh coriander leaves to garnish
a pinch of kesar (saffron)

1. Beat well curd, cream and lemon juice together.
2. Add all other ingredients except saffron.
3. Marinate chicken in this mixture for 1-2 hours.
4. Soak saffron in 1 tbsp hot water for 5 minutes. Add to the chicken.
5. Micro high covered for 10 minutes. Stir once after 5 minutes.
6. Let it stand for 2-3 minutes. Discard bay leaf and serve hot garnished with garam masala and chopped coriander leaves.

Tandoori Chicken

Serves 4-5

11"-12" ROUND MICROWAVABLE PLATE

1 chicken (600-700 gms)
1 tsp garlic paste
1 tsp ginger paste
1 tsp salt
1 tsp red chilli powder
½ tsp jeera (cumin) powder
6 tbsp curd
a little tandoori (orange red) colour
2 tbsp maida (flour)
some oil

GARNISHING
some onion rings & lemon pieces

1. Cut chicken into 8 pieces.
2. In a bowl mix all ingredients except oil.
3. Add chicken and mix well. Let it marinate for 2-3 hours at room temperature.
4. Place chicken pieces on the plate with the fleshy parts to the outside of the plate & leave extra marinade behind.
5. Dribble or brush some oil. Micro high uncovered for 4 minutes.
6. Overturn the chicken pieces. Dribble little oil on top and again micro high uncovered for 3 minutes. Let it stand for 1-2 minutes and test.
7. If need be, Micro high uncovered for 1 minute. (This is sometimes needed depending on the size the chicken and its moisture content. Check only after standing time). Garnish with onion rings and lemon & serve hot.

Note: Fish can be done in the same way.

If combination present, place chicken pieces on the metal rack. Cook in combination at 230^0C for 15 minutes. Overturn again, dribble little oil and cook in combination at 230^0C for 10 minutes.

Mughlai Vegetable Curry

Picture on back cover   *Serves 4*

6"-7" ROUND, 4-5" DEEP DISH

¼ of a small cauliflower (8 small flowerets of ½" size)
1 carrot - cut into 1/8" thick round slices
10 french beans - cut into ½" pieces
1 capsicum - cut into ½" cubes
50 gm paneer - cut into ½" cubes
2 onions, ½ " piece ginger, 3-4 flakes garlic - grind to a paste
1 tsp dhania powder
3/4 tsp jeera - crushed to a powder
½ tsp garam masala powder
¼-½ tsp red chilli powder
2 tbsp ghee or oil
3/4 cup ready made tomato puree
1½ tsp salt, or to taste

2 laung (cloves) - crushed to a powder
seeds of 1 chhoti illaichi - crushed
1½ cups milk (cold)
some chopped coriander leaves

1. Cut all the vegetables into ½" pieces. Wash cauliflower, carrots and beans. Microwave together on high for 3 minutes in a plastic bag or a covered dish. Keep aside.
2. Grind together onion, ginger and garlic to a paste.
3. Put onion paste in the dish. Sprinkle oil on it. Add jeera powder, garam masala powder, dhania powder & red chilli powder. Mix well. Micro high uncovered for 7 minutes.
4. Add tomato puree, all microwaved vegetables and capsicum. Mix well.
5. Micro high covered for 4 minutes.
6. Add paneer, salt, laung and chhoti illaichi. Mix well. Add cold milk and mix well. Keep aside till serving time.
7. At the time of serving, micro high for 3 minutes. Sprinkle chopped coriander leaves.

Shahi Machhi Patiala

Serves 3-4

8" ROUND, 3" DEEP DISH

500 gms fish (preferably skinless & boneless) - cut into 2" pieces
(but fish with skin and bones can also be used)
4 tbsp oil
1 large onion - chopped very fine (1 cup)
2-3 green chillies
½ tsp garlic paste
½ tsp ginger paste
½ tsp haldi (turmeric powder)
½ tsp red chilli powder
½ tsp salt
3 medium tomatoes - chopped very fine (2½ cups)
¾ cup water
2 heaped tsp cornflour

GRIND TOGETHER
1 tsp rai (mustard seeds)
¼ tsp ajwain
1 tsp jeera

GARNISHING
some pepper powder, some fresh coriander leaves

1. In a casserole take oil. Add powdered rai, jeera and ajwain. Micro high uncovered for 2 minutes.
2. Add haldi, onion, ginger, garlic and green chillies. Mix well. Micro high uncovered for 4 minutes.
3. Add red chilli powder, salt, tomatoes and ¾ cup water. Micro high covered for 8 minutes. Mix and mash well with a spoon.
4. Add cornflour dissolved in 2 tbsp water and fish pieces. Mix well.
5. Micro high covered for 5 minutes.
6. Let it stand for 3-4 minutes covered.
7. Serve hot garnished with fresh coriander and pepper powder.

Paneer Hara Pyaz

Picture on facing page   *Serves 4-5*

200 gm paneer- cut into 1" cubes
150 gm hare pyaz (spring onions)
1 green chilli - deseeded & chopped
3 tbsp oil
6-8 flakes garlic - crushed
¼ tsp haldi, 2 tsp dhania powder
¾ cup tomato puree (readymade)
1 tbsp tomato ketchup
3 laung (cloves) - crushed
½ tsp red chilli powder
½ tsp garam masala
½ tsp salt
4 tbsp cream or well beaten thin malai

1. Cut white of spring onions into rings, greens into ½" diagonal pieces.
2. Put oil, garlic, white of onion, haldi and dhania powder in a micro proof dish. Micro high for 5 minutes.
3. Add tomato puree, tomato ketchup, laung, red chilli powder, garam masala and salt. Mix well. Micro high for 5 minutes.
4. Add ½ cup water. Mix paneer, green chillies, cream and about 1 cup of greens of spring onions. Mix well. Micro high for 2 minutes. Serve.

Kadhai Paneer

Serves 4

6" ROUND, 3" DEEP DISH WITH COVER

200 gms paneer - cut in 1" cubes, 1 capsicum - cut into thin long strips
2 tbsp oil, 5-6 flakes garlic - crushed
4 tbsp ready made tomato puree
1 tbsp kasoori methi (dry fenugreek leaves)
1 tsp salt, ½ tsp sugar, ¾ tsp red chilli powder (to taste)
1 tsp dhania powder, ½ tsp garam masala

1. In a dish add oil and garlic. Micro high uncovered for 2 minutes.
2. Add tomato puree & kasoori methi. Add salt, sugar, red chilli powder, dhania and garam masala. Mix well. Add capsicum. Mix. Micro high uncovered for 3 minutes.
3. Add paneer. Mix well. Keep aside. At serving time, micro high covered for 2 minutes. Serve hot.

KHOYA MATAR

An excellent preparation!

Picture on page 85   *Serves 3-4*

6"-7" ROUND DISH, 2" HIGH WITH COVER

100 gms khoya - grated
1 cup matar (shelled peas)
3 tbsp oil or 2 tbsp desi ghee
1 medium sized onion
1-2 green chillies
½" piece ginger
3 tbsp ready made tomato puree
¼ - ½ tsp red chilli powder
½ tsp jeera (cumin) powder
½ tsp garam masala powder
a few cashewnuts - optional
¾ tsp salt

1. In a dish, micro high uncovered oil for 2 minutes.
2. Grind together onion, green chillies and ginger. Add onion paste to oil. Mix well.
3. Micro high uncovered for 4 minutes.
4. Add tomato puree, garam masala, red chilli powder, jeera powder, peas and 3-4 tbsp water. Mix well.
5. Micro high uncovered for 3 minutes.
6. Add salt, grated khoya, 6-7 tbsp water and cashewnuts. Mix gently so as not to mash the khoya.
7. Micro high covered for 2 minutes.
8. Serve hot.

Murg Haryali

Chicken in green masala.

Serves 4-5

8"-9" ROUND DISH, 3" DEEP WITH COVER

1 chicken (600-700 gms) - cut into 8 pieces
4-5 green chillies
¼ cup (packed) coriander leaves
¼ cup (packed) mint (poodina) leaves
2 sticks celery (optional)
2 tbsp lemon juice
2 spring onions - chopped or thinly sliced, along with the greens
2 tsp garlic paste
1½" ginger piece - grated
2 tbsp oil
1 tsp jeera (cumin) powder
1 tsp salt

1. Grind together poodina, green chillies, celery, coriander leaves to a green paste. Use lemon juice if required to grind to a paste.
2. In the dish add oil, green paste and all other ingredients, except chicken. Mix well.
3. Add chicken. Mix well.
4. Micro high uncovered for 6 minutes.
5. Mix well again. Micro high uncovered for 4 minutes.
6. Let it stand for 2 minutes.
7. Mix well. Sprinkle some garam masala and chopped coriander.
8. Serve hot, (for reheating, Micro high uncovered for 2 minutes).

Note: A combination of herbs of your choice can be used (Basil, oregano, chives, coriander, mint etc.) to make the green paste.

MIXED MASALA SUBZI

Serves 4

8-9" ROUND, 2" HIGH DISH.

4 small carrots - cut into small even sized pieces
100 gm (25-30) french beans - threaded & cut into ¼" pieces
2 onions - chopped
2 tomatoes - chopped
½ tsp haldi
½ tsp red chilli powder
½ tsp garam masala
1 tsp dhania powder
1 tsp salt or to taste
2 laung (cloves) - crushed
50 gms khoya - grated (optional)

1. Wash chopped beans and carrots. Transfer to a flat micro proof dish. Cover and micro high for 5 minutes without adding any water or till vegetables turn soft. Remove from dish.
2. Micro high 2 tbsp oil in the same dish for 2 minutes.
3. Add haldi, red chilli, garam masala, dhania and salt. Mix well. Add onions and micro high for 4 minutes.
4. Add the cooked beans and carrots. Mix in the tomatoes. Cover and micro high for 6-7 minutes.
5. Remove from microwave. Sprinkle 2 tbsp grated khoya and keep aside.
6. At serving time, micro high for 2 minutes. Serve.

Chicken Pulao

Serves 4-5

9" ROUND, 3" DEEP DISH WITH COVER

1½ cups basmati rice
4 pieces of chicken (2 legs & 2 thighs or 2 legs & 2 breasts)
2 medium sized onions - sliced thinly
4 laung (cloves)
1" stick dalchini (cinnamon)
2 moti illaichi
3 tbsp pure ghee
2 medium size tomatoes - chopped finely
2 tsp salt
1 tsp garam masala
1 tsp red chilli powder
1 tsp garlic paste, 1 tsp ginger paste
2½ cups water

1. Wash and soak the rice in water for 1 hour.
2. In the dish, add ghee, onion, moti illaichi, laung and dalchini. Micro high uncovered for 3 minutes.
3. Add rice, chicken, tomatoes, salt, garam masala, red chillies, garlic and ginger paste. Mix well.
4. Add 2½ cups water. Mix.
5. Micro high covered for 17 minutes.
6. Let it stand for 4-5 minutes. Fluff it up with a fork to separate the grains of rice.
7. Serve hot.

Note: When you finish cooking, some water may still remain in the rice but it is absorbed during standing time as cooking process still continues for a while, even after the rice is removed from the microwave.

Spinach & Corn Pullao

The green spinach makes a very appealing combination with yellow corn and some red shreds of carrot. The fennel seeds (saunf) adds to the delightful flavour.

Serves 4

9-10" ROUND, 2-3" HIGH DISH

150 gm spinach (palak) - leaves cut into thin strips (2 cups)
½ cup cooked or tinned corn kernels
1 carrot - grated thickly
1 cup basmati rice - washed and kept moist in the strainer for 1 hour
2 tbsp desi ghee or oil
1 tsp saunf
2 moti illaichi (brown cardamoms)
1" stick dalchini (cinnamon), 2 laung (cloves)
1 onion - chopped finely
1½ tsp salt

¼ tsp red chilli powder
2 green chillies

1. Wash rice. Strain and let it be in the strainer for 1 hour.
2. Put ghee in a big, flat dish. Add saunf. Mix well. Add moti illaichi, dalchini and laung. Mix well with the ghee. Add onions. Micro high uncovered all together for 3 minutes.
3. Add washed and drained spinach, corn & grated carrots. Micro high uncovered for 2 minutes.
4. Add the rice to the spinach.
5. Add salt and red chilli powder. Add 2 cups water. Mix very well, but gently.
6. Micro high covered for 12 minutes. Stir once in-between after 5 minutes with a fork.
7. Let it stand for 2 minutes. Fluff it up with a fork to separate the grains. Serve hot.

KADHAI CHICKEN

Serves 4

8" ROUND, 3" DEEP DISH WITH COVER

Chicken (450 - 500 gms) with or without bones - cut into pieces of your choice
3 tbsp oil
1 tsp garlic paste
½ cup ready made tomato puree (Godrej or Kissan)
½ tsp red chilli powder
1 tsp dhania powder, ½ tsp garam masala
1 tsp sugar
a little orange red colour
1 tsp salt
2 large capsicums - cut into strips
3 tsp cornflour dissolved in 3 tsp water

GARNISHING
some kasoori methi

1. In the dish, mix oil, garlic paste and chicken. Micro high covered for 4 minutes.
2. Add tomato puree and all other ingredients except the last three- salt, capsicum and cornflour. Mix well.
3. Micro high covered for 4 minutes.
4. Add capsicum strips, salt and cornflour dissolved in 3 tsp water. Mix well.
5. Micro high uncovered for 3 minutes.
6. Let it stand for 1-2 minutes.
7. Mix. Sprinkle some kasoori methi on top and serve hot.

Matar waale Chaawal

Serves 4

9-10" ROUND, 2-3 " HIGH DISH

1 cup basmati rice - soaked for 1 hour
1 cup shelled peas, 3 tbsp oil
½" piece ginger - grated , 1 large onion- sliced finely
1½ tsp salt, ¼ tsp red chilli powder, ¼ tsp garam masala , 2-3 laung (cloves)
2 green chillies, 2 tbsp chopped coriander
1 firm tomato - cut into strips & pulp removed

1. Micro high oil in a large dish for 2 minutes.
2. Add peas, onions, ginger, salt, chilli powder, garam masala & laung. Micro high for 3 minutes.
3. Drain the rice and add to it. Add 2 cups water, whole green chillies, coriander leaves and tomato strips. Mix lightly.
4. Micro high for 11 minutes. Stir once after 5 minutes.
5. Let it stand for 2 minutes. Fluff it up with a fork to separate the grains. Serve hot.

Khatte Mithe Baingan

Picture on cover   Serves 4-5

7" - 8" ROUND DISH, 1-2 " HIGH WITH COVER

300 gm small baingans, 4-5 thick green or red chillies, 3 tbsp oil

STUFFING

2 tsp til (sesame seeds), 2 tsp oil
1¼ tsp salt, 1½ tsp amchoor, ½ tsp haldi, ¾ tsp sugar
½ tsp red chilli powder, ½ tsp garam masala, 2 tsp dhania powder

1. Wash, slit brinjals, making cross cuts. Slit green chillies. Deseed them.
2. Mix til, salt, sugar, chilli powder, garam masala, amchoor, dhania powder and haldi together. Add 2 tsp oil and mix.
3. Fill the paste in the baingans and green chillies.
4. Arrange in a dish. Pour oil on them. Micro high covered for 8 minutes. Let it stand for 2-3 minutes. Check if soft. Microwave for a minute or two more if not done. Serve hot.

Prawn Malai Curry

Delicious, creamy prawns!

Picture on facing page   *Serves 4*

500 gm prawns - shelled and cleaned
3 onions - chopped finely
1 tsp jeera powder
½ tsp red chilli paste
1 tbsp ginger paste
1 tbsp garlic paste
1 tsp haldi
1 tsp garam masala powder
½ cup cream
salt to taste
3 tbsp oil
2 green chillies - chopped finely

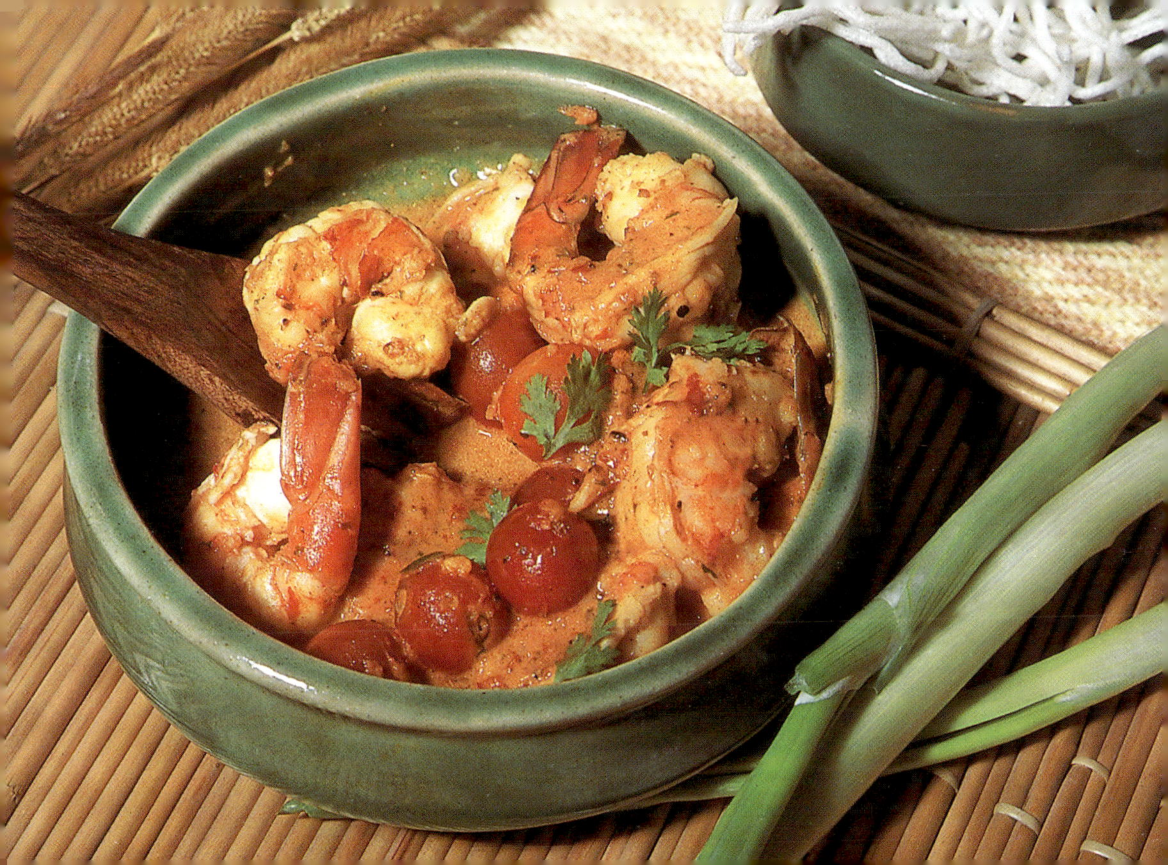

1. Clean, de-vein and wash prawns. Apply salt.
2. Chop onions finely. Chop green chillies.
3. Combine ghee and onions in casserole. Add jeera powder, red chilli paste, ginger-garlic paste, haldi and half the garam masala powder. Microwave high for 6 minutes.
4. Stir in prawns and 1 cup water. Cover and microwave high for 7 minutes.
5. Blend cream in and microwave high for 1 minute.
6. Sprinkle with remaining garam masala powder and garnish with green chillies.

Dal Maharani

Serves 4

7-8" ROUND, 4-5" DEEP DISH WITH A WELL FITTING LID

1 cup dhuli urad dal (split black beans) - soaked for 1 hour
1 onion - sliced
1" piece ginger - grated
3 tbsp oil
1¼ tsp salt, ½ tsp haldi
½ tsp red chilli powder, ¼ tsp amchoor, ¼ tsp dhania powder

1. Clean and wash dal. Soak in water for 1 hour.
2. Keep onion and ginger in a dish. Sprinkle oil on it. Mix. Add salt, haldi, chilli powder, amchoor and dhania powder. Micro high uncovered for 5 minutes.
3. Drain the dal and add to the onions. Add 2 cups water. Mix well. Micro high covered for 20 minutes. Stir once after 8 minutes in-between. Let it stand 3 minutes. Sprinkle chopped coriander & mix gently with a fork.

Chicken & Paneer Shashlik

Makes 6 skewers (Serves 6)

8" ROUND, 1-2" HIGH DISH

250 gm paneer - cut into large (1½") cubes and brushed with some oil
1 large capsicum - cut into large cubes
8 cherry tomatoes or 1 large tomato - cut into 8 pieces & pulp removed
200 gm boneless chicken - cut into 1½" pieces (12 pieces) or 12 big mushrooms
1 large onion - cut into 8 pieces & separated
some chat masala to sprinkle

MARINADE

1 cup thick curd - hung for 30 minutes
2 tbsp fresh cream, 2 tbsp almonds - ground to a rough powder
2 tsp kasoori methi, 1 tsp cornflour, 1 tbsp thick ginger-garlic paste
½ tsp black salt, ¼ tsp haldi, 2 tsp tandoori masala
½ tsp red chilli powder, 1 tsp salt or to taste

SAUCE

2 tbsp butter, 4-5 flakes garlic - crushed
3/4 cup ready made tomato puree, ¼ tsp red chilli paste or powder
½ tsp worcestershire sauce, ½ tsp soya sauce
½ tsp pepper, ¾ tsp salt or to taste, ¼ tsp sugar, ½ cup water
2-3 tbsp fresh cream (added later)

RICE TO SERVE

1 cup rice mixed with 2 chhoti illaichi, 1-2 blades javetri, 1 tsp salt , 1 tbsp lemon juice and 2 cups water and microwaved covered for 12 minutes

1. Mix all ingredients of the marinade in a large bowl. Add chicken first and mix well to coat the marinade. Keep in the marinade for atleast 2 hours or till serving time. At serving time, remove chicken from bowl. Add paneer. Coat and remove from bowl. Similarly, coat the onion and capsicum together, and finally tomatoes.

2. Arrange them on greased wooden skewers. Micro high skewers for 6 minutes, turning once in between and pour a little oil on them also. If you do not posses skewers, place the marinated vegetables directly on a flat plate.

3. For the sauce, micro high butter and garlic for 2 minutes. Stir. Add all other ingredients except cream. Mix and micro high for 4 minutes or till it boils, stirring once in between. Remove from oven. Add cream to the sauce.
4. To serve, spread some rice on a plate. Keeping the vegetable skewers on the rice, pull out the skewers carefully to get an arranged line of vegetables on the rice. Do it with all the skewers. Pour the sauce over the vegetables and rice. Micro high for 2 minutes. Serve hot sprinkled with chaat masala.

CONTINENTAL, CHINESE & THAI

Fish in Herb Sauce

A delicious aromatic dish!

Serves 3-4

1 LARGE ROUND PLATE AND 1 CASSEROLE LARGE ENOUGH TO ACCOMMODATE FISH IN A SINGLE LAYER

500 gms fish - cut into 5-6 pieces
1 tsp ginger paste
1 tsp garlic paste
3-4 green chillies - cut very finely or minced
½-1 tsp salt or to taste
2 tsp lemon juice
½ tsp ajwain
½ tsp pepper

SAUCE
2 tbsp fresh coriander leaves
18-20 poodina (mint) leaves

2 tsp lemon juice
½ tsp salt
½ cup water
1 tsp cornflour dissolved in 1 tbsp water

1. Mix all the ingredients given under fish. Rub them well over the fish. Place in a dish in a single layer.
2. Micro high uncovered for 2 minutes. Turn over fish with tongs or spoon. Again mirco high uncovered 2 minutes.
3. Remove fish to a plate.
4. In the dish in which fish was cooked (there may be some juices present) add all ingredients under ingredients for sauce. Mix well.
5. Micro high uncovered for 2 minutes, stir once after 1 minute.
6. Spoon this sauce over fish. Cover and Micro high for 2 minutes. Serve hot.

Note: Prawns or Paneer pieces can be used, instead of fish.

Garlic Chicken

Serves 2-3

8" ROUND, 3" DEEP DISH WITH COVER

200 gms chicken - cut into bite size pieces (can be boneless or with bones)
3 tbsp oil
2-3 dried red chillies - broken into pieces and deseeded
2 tbsp finely chopped garlic
1 tsp red chilli powder
1 cup tomato puree
1-2 tsp sugar (according to taste)
1 tsp soya sauce
¼ tsp ajinomoto (optional)
½ tsp salt
1½ tbsp cornflour dissolved in 7-8 tbsp water (increase water if more gravy is desired)
1 tsp sherry (optional)

1. In the dish, mix oil, broken red chillies, red chilli powder and chopped garlic. Micro high for 3 minutes uncovered.
2. Add chicken and all other ingredients except cornflour.
3. Micro high covered for 5 minutes.
4. Add cornflour paste. Mix well. Micro high uncovered for 3 minutes or till sauce boils.
5. Let it stand for 2-3 minutes. Mix well before serving.

Chicken a' la Kiev

Serves 4-5

10" ROUND, 4" DEEP DISH WITH COVER

1 chicken (600-700 gms) - cut into small pieces
18-20 french beans - cut into 1½" pieces
2 medium carrots - cut into 1½" pieces
2 sticky celery - chopped fine
2 capsicums - cut into ¼" pieces
½ cup milk
2 level tbsp maida
1 tsp pepper
1 tsp mustard powder
1 tsp salt
4 tbsp grated cheese (Amul)

1. In a casserole mix together chicken, carrots, celery and french beans. Add 2-3 tbsp water, cover.
2. Micro high covered for 5 minutes.
3. Mix maida with milk so that no lumps remain. Add to chicken.
4. Add pepper, mustard, salt and capsicum.
5. Mix well. Micro high covered for 4 minutes.
6. Stir once after 2 minutes otherwise maida tends to settle down.
7. Add cheese (grated). Mix well.
8. Micro high covered for 3 minutes.
9. Let it stand for 1-2 minutes. Mix. Serve garnished with parsley or coriander.

Note: Vegetables of your choice can be used.

Macaroni Cheese

Serves 3-4

5-6" ROUND DISH, 4-5" DEEP

1 cup uncooked macaroni (small)
2 tbsp butter
1 onion or 2 spring onions - chopped along with green parts
2½ tbsp flour (maida)
1¾ cups milk
¾ tsp salt
½ tsp pepper
¼ tsp mustard powder
25 gm cheese (1 cube) - grated
1 tbsp bread crumbs
some tomato slices & chopped coriander leaves

1. Micro high 1½ cups of water with 1 tsp oil in a medium sized deep dish uncovered for 3 minutes.
2. Add macaroni. Micro high uncovered for 5 minutes.
3. Let it stand in hot water for 4-5 minutes. Drain and wash well with cold water.
4. In a clean dish, micro high butter for 1 minute.
5. Add spring onions and micro high covered for 2 minutes.
6. Add flour. Mix well and Micro high uncovered for 30 seconds.
7. Add milk. Stir well, so that no lumps are formed.
8. Add salt, pepper and Micro high uncovered for 3 minutes stirring after every minute to avoid lump formation. Microwave for 1-2 minutes more if the sauce does not turn thick.
9. Add mustard powder, boiled macaroni, grated cheese. Mix well.
10. Sprinkle bread crumbs on top. Arrange 2-3 tomato slices and sprinkle a little chopped coriander. Micro high uncovered for 2 minutes. Serve.

Penne & Rice Baked in Spinach Sauce

Picture on page 1   *Serves 5-6*

7" ROUND DISH, 2" HIGH

1 cup uncooked penne pasta (diagonally cut tubes)
1½ cups cooked rice - white or brown mixed with ¼ cup chopped parsley
100 gm mushrooms or baby corns - sliced
2 tbsp butter, 1 cup finely chopped spinach
2½ tbsp flour (maida), 2½ - 3 cups milk
¾ tsp salt, or to taste, 1 tsp pepper
1½ tsp oregano
100 gm mozzarella cheese - grated (1½ cups)
2 tbsp bread crumbs
some tomato slices & black olives

1. Micro high 2½ cups of water with 1 tsp oil and 1 tsp salt in a medium sized deep dish uncovered for 4 minutes.

2. Add penne. Micro high uncovered for 8 minutes. Let it stand in hot water for 4-5 minutes. Drain and wash well with cold water.
3. In a clean dish, micro high butter for 1 minute.
4. Add oregano, spinach, mushrooms or baby corns and micro high uncovered for 5 minutes.
5. Add flour. Mix well and micro high uncovered for 30 seconds.
6. Add milk. Stir well, so that no lumps are formed.
7. Add salt, pepper and micro high uncovered for 4 minutes stirring once in between to avoid lump formation. Microwave for 1-2 minutes more if the sauce does not turn thick.
8. Add penne and ¼ cup of the grated cheese. Mix well. Keep aside.
9. Spread parsley rice in a clean greased dish. Push them toward the edges of the dish to get a rice border. Sprinkle ½ cup grated cheese on it. Leaving aside the border of rice spread the pasta over the center portion of the rice, such that the rice border shows. Sprinkle bread crumbs on top. Arrange 2-3 tomato slices and sprinkle the left over grated cheese. Scatter a few sliced olives. Dot with butter.
10. At serving time micro high uncovered for 4 minutes. Serve.

Hungarian Paneer

A quick and attractive way of serving paneer.

Picture on facing page Serves 8

700-800 gm paneer - cut into a long, thick slab (7" long and 2" thick, approx.)

FILLING (MIX TOGETHER)
¼ cup grated carrot (½ carrot), ½ cup grated cabbage
2 tbsp grated cheese
¼ tsp salt and ¼ tsp freshly ground pepper, ½ tsp oregano, or to taste

HUNGARIAN SAUCE
5 tomatoes
6 tbsp ready made tomato puree
2 tbsp oil, 1 tsp crushed garlic (6-8 flakes)
1 tsp oregano
½ tsp salt and ¼ tsp pepper, or to taste
4 tbsp cream

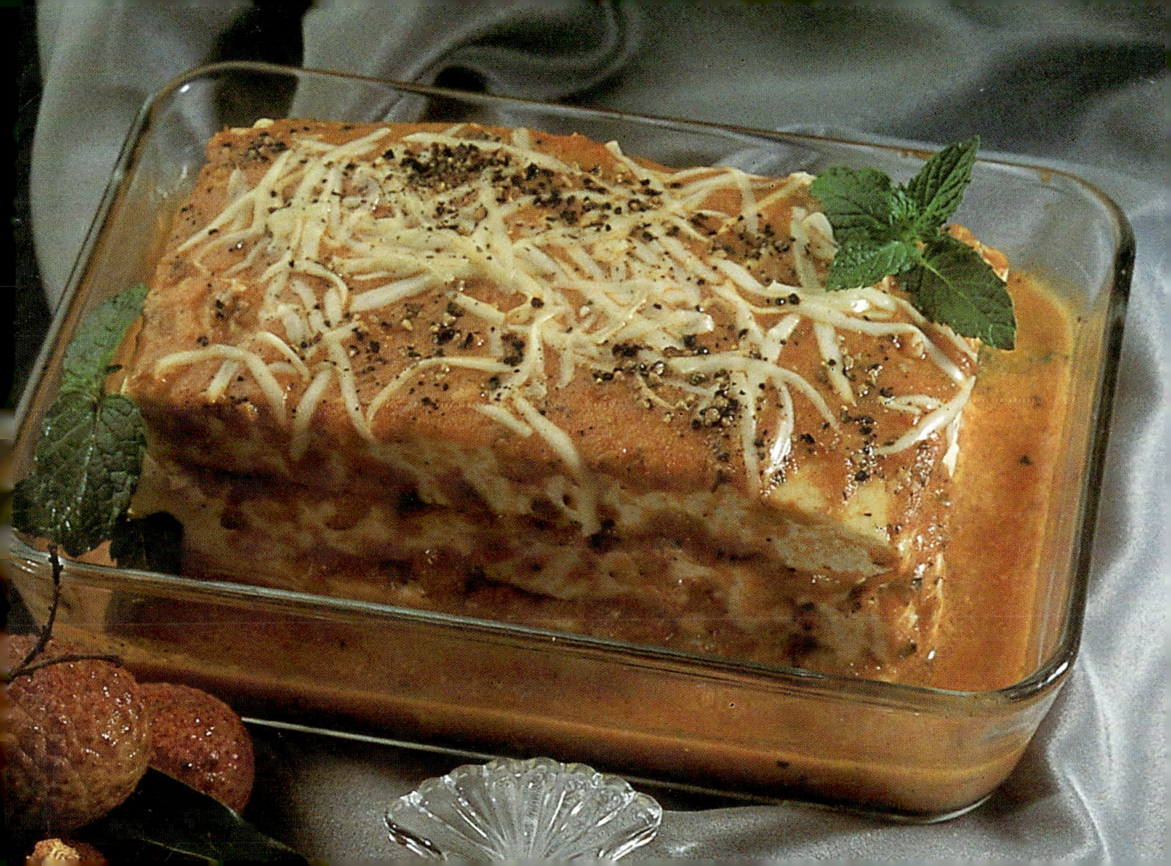

1. To prepare the sauce, wash and microwave tomatoes in ¾ cup water for 4 minutes till soft. Remove from oven. Remove tomatoes from water. Peel them and blend to a puree when cold. Keep fresh tomato puree aside.
2. Micro high oil, garlic, 6 tbsp tomato puree and oregano for 2 minutes.
3. Add the prepared fresh tomato puree and micro high for 4 minutes. Remove from oven. Add salt and pepper to taste.
4. Mix in cream and keep the sauce aside.
5. Cut paneer into 3 equal pieces lengthwise. Sprinkle salt and pepper on both sides of each slice of paneer.
6. In a shallow rectangular serving dish, put ¼ of the prepared sauce.
7. Place a paneer slab on the sauce.
8. Spread ½ of the carrot-cabbage filling on it.
9. Press another piece of paneer on it.
10. Again put the filling on it. Cover with the last piece of paneer. Press.
11. Pour the sauce all over the paneer to cover the top and the sides completely. Grate cheese on top. Sprinkle some oregano or pepper.
12. Cover loosely with a cling film and micro high for 3 minutes.

Chicken Stroganoff

Serves 4-6

2 LITRE CASSEROLE DISH

1 kg chicken - deboned and sliced into thin strips, 1 tsp worcestershire sauce
¼ cup maida (plain flour), ¼ cup cold water
300 ml (1½ cups) chicken stock or 1½ cups water mixed with 1 chicken seasoning cube
100 gm button mushrooms
1¼ tsp salt, or to taste, ¼ tsp pepper
¾ cup sour cream, 1 tbsp tomato sauce (optional)

1. Place chicken and worcestershire sauce in a 2 litre casserole dish. Microwave high for 10 minutes.
2. Blend flour and cold water. Stir into chicken.
3. Add stock. Stir in mushrooms, salt and pepper. Microwave high for 10 minutes, stirring once in between.
4. Blend in sour cream and tomato sauce. Serve over noodles or rice.

Chicken with Mushrooms & Baby Corn

Serves 4-5

9" ROUND, 3" DEEP DISH WITH COVER

200 gms chicken - cut into bite size pieces
100 gms mushrooms - sliced
100 gms baby corn - sliced diagonally
1 tsp garlic paste
1 tsp ginger paste
2 tbsp oil
1 tbsp soya sauce
1 tbsp vinegar
1¼ tsp salt
1¼ tsp pepper
2 tbsp cornflour
¼ tsp ajinomoto (optional)

1. In the casserole mix together oil, ginger paste, garlic paste and chicken.
2. Micro high covered for 4 minutes.
3. Add mushrooms, baby corn and all other ingredients except cornflour. Add ½ cup water.
4. Mix well. Micro high covered for 3 minutes.
5. Mix cornflour in 1 cup water. Add to cooked chicken mixture. Mix well.
6. Micro high uncovered for 2 minutes or till sauce boils. Let it stand for 2 minutes. Serve hot.

Note: If less gravy (sauce) is desired, dissolve cornflour in ½ cup water and reduce salt and pepper to 1 tsp each.

Chicken Hong Kong

Delicious, dry, spicy dish.

Serves 3-4

6" ROUND, 3" DEEP DISH WITH COVER, 6" ROUND PLATE

300 gms chicken - cut into bite size pieces *(can be boneless or with bones)*
3 tbsp soya sauce
3 tsp sherry (optional)
½ tsp salt, ½ tsp sugar
½ tsp ajinomoto (optional)
15-16 cashew nuts - halved
6 dried, broken, deseeded red chillies
1 tsp red chilli powder
2-3 flakes garlic - crushed or chopped very fine
2 tbsp oil
2 level tsp cornflour dissolved in 1 tbsp water

1. In a dish, mix chicken, soya sauce, sherry, salt, sugar and ajinomoto. Leave to marinate for 1-1½ hours.
2. In a casserole add oil, broken, dried red chillies, chilli powder & garlic.
3. Micro high uncovered for 2 minutes.
4. In a plate place cashew nuts in a single layer. Micro high (dry) uncovered for 2 minutes to roast nuts. Stir once after 1 minute.
5. To the casserole of stage 2, add chicken and all the marinade. Mix well.
6. Micro high covered for 4 minutes.
7. Dissolve cornflour in 1 tbsp water. Add to chicken. Add roasted cashewnuts. Mix well.
8. Micro high uncovered for 2 minutes.
9. Let it stand for 1-2 minutes. Serve hot.

Stuffed Tomatoes

Serves 5-6

5 large or 6 medium sized tomatoes
1 cup cottage cheese (paneer) - mashed roughly
½ cup onion - chopped fine
½ cup capsicum - chopped fine
½ cup boiled green peas
2 tbsp tomato ketchup
2 tbsp chilli sauce
¾ tsp salt
½ tsp garam masala
1 tsp amchoor (dried mango powder) powder
coriander leaves

1. Cut tomatoes into 2 halves. Remove pulp and keep inverted for 3-4 minutes.
2. Mix all other ingredients well.
3. Spoon filling into tomato halves and place in a ring on a plate in the microwave.
4. Micro high uncovered for 2-3 minutes or until tomatoes are tender.
5. If combination present instead of step 4 keep tomatoes in combination 5 minutes.
6. Allow to stand for 2 minutes. Serve hot garnished with coriander leaves.

Note: Lightly score the tomato skin so as to prevent the tomatoes from splitting.

Variation:

Stuffed capsicums can be made in the same way. Filling of your choice can be used.

Thai Green Chicken Curry

Picture on facing page   *Serve 5-6*

9" ROUND, 3" DEEP DISH WITH COVER

GREEN PASTE
(Grind together with a little water)
6-8 green chillies
3 spring onions chopped along with the green part (or 2 small button onions)
4 lemon grass leaves - optional
2" piece ginger, 3 tbsp coriander leaves

MAIN DISH
1 chicken (700-800 gms) - cut into pieces of your choice
1½ cups coconut milk
1½ tsp salt
a tiny piece of gur (jaggery)
1 tbsp dhania (coriander) powder, 1 tbsp jeera (cumin) powder
2 tbsp oil

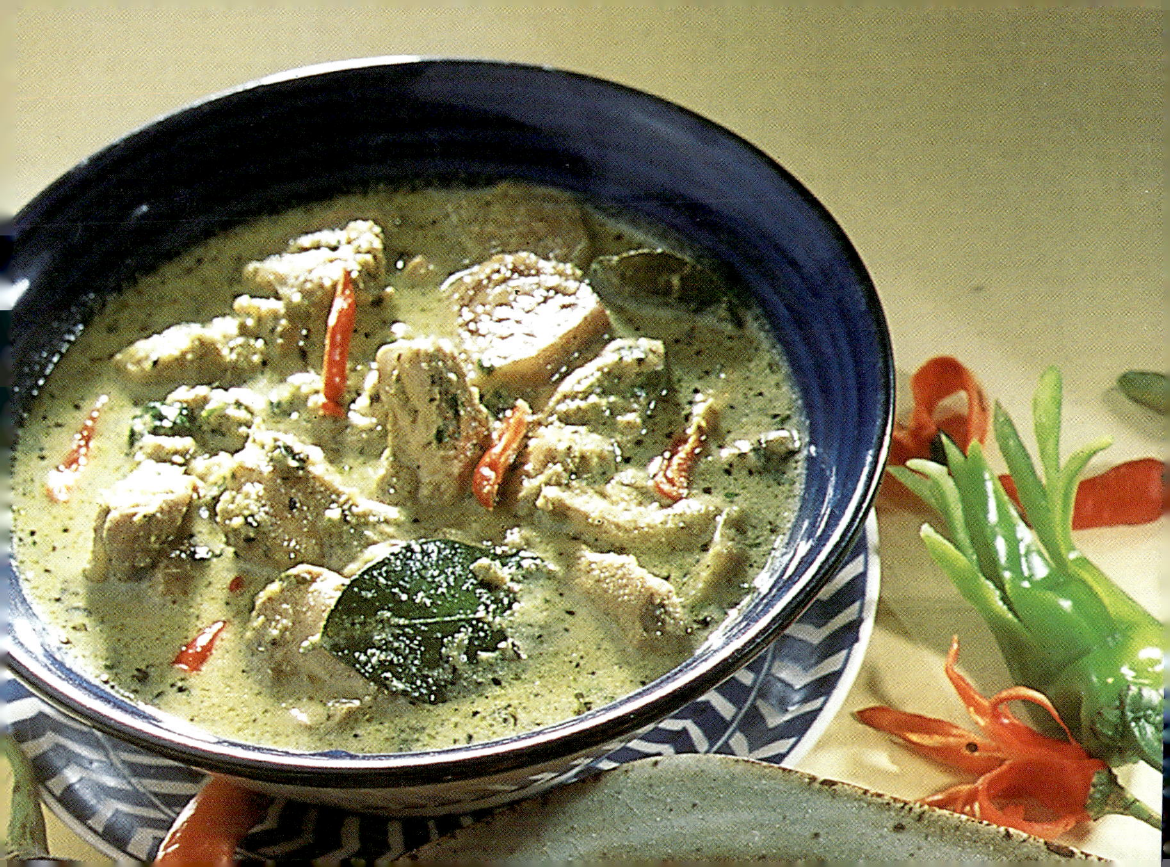

1. Prepare the green paste by grinding everything together given under the green paste in the grinder. Use little water if required for grinding.
2. Grate one coconut. Soak in 1½ cups of warm water for 1-2 hours.
3. Churn in the mixer and strain to extract coconut milk.
4. In a dish add oil, green paste, coriander and jeera powder. Mix well.
5. Micro high uncovered for 3 minutes.
6. Add chicken. Mix well.
7. Micro high covered for 4 minutes.
8. Add salt, jaggery and coconut milk. Mix well so that jaggery dissolves.
9. Micro high uncovered for 3 minutes.
10. Let it stand for 2-3 minutes.
11. Serve garnished with chopped red chillies or coriander or basil leaves

Note:
1. This dish is supposed to be very hot. If a lesser hot dish is desired, reduce green chillies to 4-5.
2. Instead of chicken, mixed vegetables can also be used.

Chilli Chicken

Serves 3-4

8" ROUND, 3" DEEP DISH WITH COVER

350 gms chicken - cut into bite size pieces *(boneless or with bones)*
½" piece ginger - chopped fine, 2-3 flakes garlic - chopped fine
1 tbsp vinegar, 2 tbsp soya sauce, ½ tsp ajinomoto (optional)
4-5 green chillies - slit length ways
1 medium capsicum - cut into thin strips
½ onion - cut into ½" thin strips and leaves separated
1 tsp sugar, 1 tsp salt, 2 tsp sherry or rum (optional)
2 tsp (level) cornflour

1. In the dish, mix oil, ajinomoto, ginger, garlic, soya sauce and chicken. Micro high covered for 4 minutes.
2. Add all ingredients including chillies, capsicum and cornflour mixed in ¼ cup water. Micro high uncovered for 2 minutes. Serve.

SNACKS

Tandoori Fish

The red colour is important to give the microwaved fish, a tandoori look.

Serves 4-5 *Picture on page 103*

11"-12" ROUND MICROWAVABLE PLATE

500 gm fish - cut into broad fingers
1 tsp garlic paste
1 tsp ginger paste
1 tsp salt
1 tsp red chilli powder
½ tsp jeera (cumin) powder
½ cup curd - hung to get about 4 tbsp thick curd
a little tandoori (orange red) colour
2 tbsp maida (flour)
some oil

GARNISHING
some onion rings & lemon pieces

1. Cut fish into 5-6 pieces.
2. In a bowl mix all ingredients except oil.
3. Add fish and mix well. Let it marinate for 2-3 hours at room temperature.
4. Place fish pieces on the plate and leave extra marinade behind.
5. Dribble some oil or brush with oil. Micro high uncovered for 4 minutes.
6. Overturn the pieces. Dribble a little oil on top again and micro high uncovered for 3 minutes. Let it stand for 1-2 minutes and test.
7. Garnish with onion rings and lemon wedges. Serve hot.

Note: If grill is present - place chicken pieces on the metal rack. Grill at 230°C for 15 minutes. Overturn, again dribble little oil and grill further for 10 minutes.

Potato Based Pizza

Serves 4

9" ROUND DISH, 1" HIGH

PIZZA BASE

100 gms maida (1 cup packed)
2 tbsp/30 gms butter
1 medium/100 gms potato
½ tsp baking powder
½ tsp salt

PIZZA SAUCE

4 tbsp ready made tomato puree
½ tsp garam masala, ½ tsp dhania powder
½ tsp oregano or ¼ tsp ajwain - powdered
½ tsp salt, 1 tsp sugar
½ tsp chilli powder

TOPPING

50 gms cheese
½ medium onion - thinly sliced
½ medium capsicum - thinly sliced

1. Put the potato in a polythene bag and Micro high for 2½ minutes. Mash the cooked potato to a smooth paste. Keep aside to cool.
2. Rub butter into the flour till it resembles bread crumbs.
3. Add mashed potato, baking powder and salt.
4. Knead to a dough using a few tbsp cold water.
5. To prepare the sauce, mix all the ingredients with the tomato puree. Keep aside.
6. Roll out pizza dough and spread out in the dish.
7. Spread sauce on the pizza, leaving ¼" space all around. Micro high uncovered for 6 minutes.
8. Mix a little salt to onion and capsicum and sprinkle on the pizza. Grate cheese on it. Micro high uncovered for 1 minute.
9. Let it stand for 2-3 minutes before slicing.

KHANDAVI

Very simple to prepare!

Makes 8 rolls

½ cup gram flour (besan)
¾ cup curd
¾ cup water
½ tsp salt, ¼ tsp haldi
pinch of hing (asafoetida)
½" piece ginger - crushed to a paste
1 green chilli - crushed to a paste

TEMPERING (BAGHAR)

1½ tbsp oil
½ tsp rai (mustard seeds) - crushed
1 green chilli - chopped fine (optional)
few coriander leaves - chopped
a little freshly grated coconut

1. Mix besan, curd and water well with a beater so that no lumps remain.
2. Pour into a dish and micro uncovered 80% power for 4 minutes.
3. Add haldi, salt, ginger chilli paste and hing.
4. Stir well and Micro high for 3 minutes or till mixture is thick.
5. Remove from microwave.
6. Mix well and spread quickly, thinly on a plastic sheet. Let it cool for 5-7 minutes. Cut into thin strips (1" broad) and make rolls.
7. For the baghar, micro high oil uncovered for 2 minutes.
8. Add rai and green chilli. Micro high uncovered for 2 minutes.
9. Add coriander leaves and coconut. Mix and pour over the prepared khandavi.

Khoya Matar: Recipe on page 32 ➤
Gajar ka Halwa: Recipe on page 95 ➤

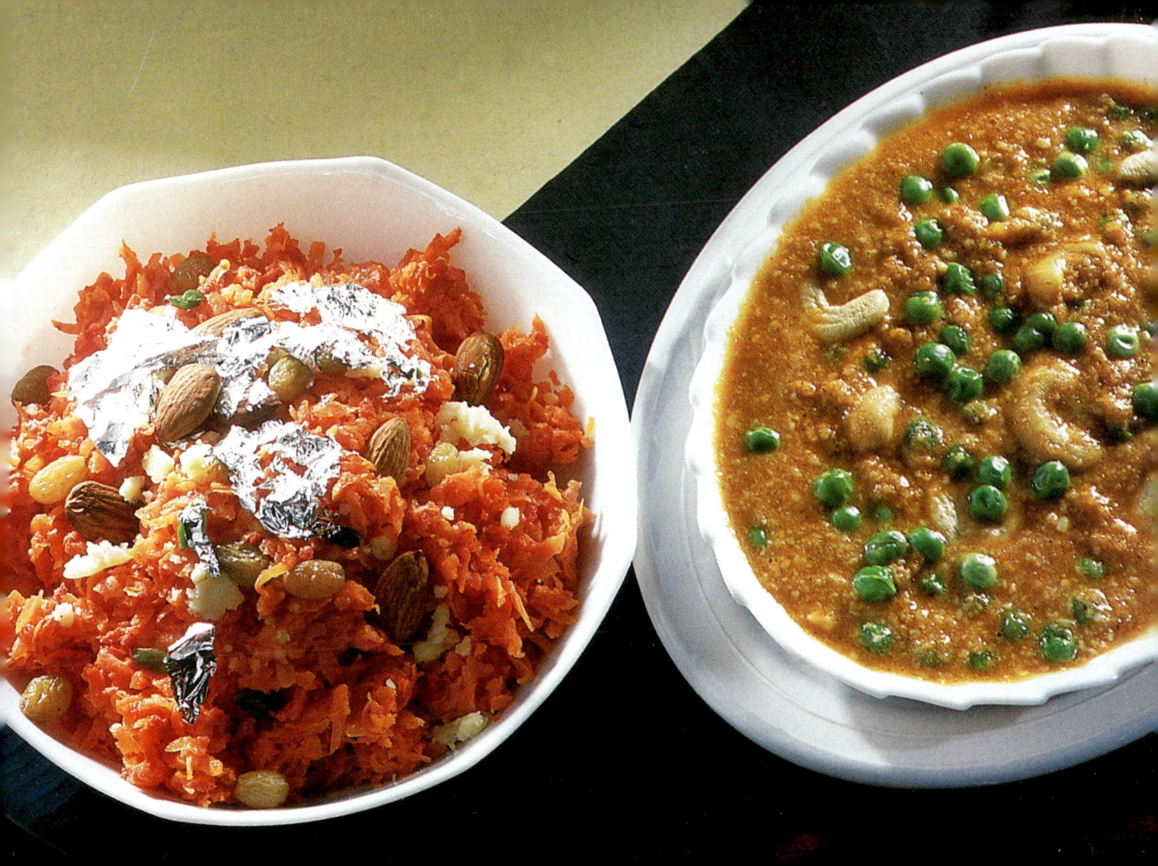

Murg Malai Kababs

Picture on page 2   *Gives 6-8 pieces*

8" ROUND 1" DEEP DISH OR ANY MICROWAVABLE PLATE

200 gms boneless (skinless) chicken - cut in 1½"- 2 " pieces

(pieces should be of even size)

1 tsp garlic paste
1 tbsp chopped coriander
½ tsp saunf (aniseed) - crushed
¾ tsp salt
1 tsp amchoor (dry mango) powder
1 tsp red chilli powder, preferably degi mirch
¼ tsp nutmeg powder
4 tbsp cream or malai
1 tbsp oil
1 tsp cornflour

1. Place chicken in a bowl. Add all the ingredients and mix well. Let it marinate for 1-2 hours at room temperature.
2. Place kababs on a plate in the form of a ring.
3. Micro high uncovered for 2 minutes.
4. Turn over (change the side) of the kababs. Again Micro high for 2 minutes.
5. Remove to a serving dish and serve hot.

Note: Check after standing time. If the kabab is not fully cooked, micro high for 1 minute more.

Some juice may remain after kababs are made. Discard it. The amount of juice will depend on the water content of the chicken.

Rawa Idli

Delicious idlis can be on the breakfast table in no time.

Makes 5 big idlis

5 SMALL GLASS (MICRO PROOF) KATORIS (BOWLS)

1 tbsp oil
1-2 green chillies
1 cup suji (rawa)
2 tbsp chopped coriander leaves
½ tsp soda-bicarb
1 cup curd
¼ cup grated coconut, optional
½ cup water
¾ tsp salt

1. Chop coriander leaves and green chillies finely.
2. In a dish micro high uncovered 1 tbsp oil for 2 minutes.
3. Add chillies. Micro high uncovered for 1 minute.
4. Add suji (rawa). Mix well. Micro high uncovered for 1 minute.
5. Add coriander leaves and salt. Mix well. Allow to cool.
6. Add coconut, curd, water and soda-bicarb. Keep aside for 10 minutes.
7. Grease small glass katoris or plastic boxes. Pour 2-3 tbsp mixture into each katori.
8. Arrange in a ring in the microwave and micro high uncovered for 4 minutes.
9. Let it stand for 5 minutes. Serve hot with coconut chutney.

Note: One idli takes 1 minute for cooking. So cooking time increases as per the number of idlis. If the idlis are made beforehand, remove from moulds and keep in a covered box. Before serving micro high for 1 minute. Idlis should always be served hot.

Ordinary idlis of rice-dal mixture can also be made similarly in a microwave.

Chicken Tikka Tandoori

Gives 10-12 pieces

8"ROUND, 1" DEEP DISH

200 gms boneless chicken - cut into 1½" - 2" pieces
1 tsp garlic paste
1 tsp ginger paste
½ tsp red chilli powder - (adjust to taste)
1 tsp salt
½ tsp garam masala powder
1 tsp amchoor powder
3 tbsp hung curd or thick curd
a little tandoori (orange red) colour
1 medium size onion - cut into quarters & leaves separated
1 medium size capsicum - cut into broad pieces
some oil - for sprinkling on tikkas

1. Hang 1 cup curd made from low fat milk for 1½-2 hours in a muslin cloth. It gives 3 tbsp hung curd or thick curd.
2. In a bowl, add chicken, onion, capsicum and all other ingredients.
3. Mix well. Marinate for 1-2 hours at room temperature.
4. Place chicken pieces on the dish. Sprinkle little oil on them. Micro high uncovered for 2 minutes. Turn over and again sprinkle little oil over them. Again Micro high for 2 minutes.
5. Remove plate from microwave and let it stand 1-2 minutes.
6. In the meantime place marinated capsicum and onion pieces on another plate. Micro high uncovered for 2 minutes.
7. On the serving plate place chicken onion & capsicum pieces alternatively.
8. Serve hot.

Note: Check after standing time. If the tikka is not fully cooked, micro high for 1 minute more.

Paneer & Grape Sticks

Cinnamon flavoured snack served with drinks.

Serves 4

3"- 4" (SMALL) ROUND BOWL

100 gms paneer - cut into ¾" cubes
15-20 grapes - washed well
2 tsp oil
a few plastic cocktail forks or wooden tooth picks

MASALA

1 stick dalchini (cinnamon)
3-4 laung (cloves)
½ tsp ajwain (carom seeds)
4-5 chhoti illaichi (green cardamoms)

1. Crush or grind all the ingredients of the masala together to a coarse powder on a chakla-belan or a small spice grinder. Keep aside.
2. Micro high oil in a small bowl for 2 minutes. Add the powdered masala. Mix well. Add the paneer pieces. Sprinkle a little salt. Mix very well. Keep aside till serving time.
3. At serving time, micro high paneer for 1 minute.
4. Insert a hot paneer piece in the tooth pick & then a grape. Serve with cold drinks before meals.

DESSERTS

Gajar ka Halwa

Picture on page 85 Serves 5-6

10" ROUND, 5" DEEP DISH

½ kg carrots - grated
1½ cups milk
½ - ¾ cup sugar - powdered
½ cup (100 gms) khoya - grated
2-3 tbsp desi ghee
some chopped nuts like almonds, raisins (kishmish) etc.

1. Mix grated carrots and milk.
2. Micro high uncovered for 15 minutes. Mix once after 5 minutes.
3. Add sugar and khoya. Mix well.
4. Micro high for 10 minutes uncovered.
5. Add ghee. Mix well. Micro high for 7 minutes. Mix chopped nuts. Serve hot or cold decorated with nuts.

Peaches in Sauce

Serves 4

6-7" ROUND, 1-1½" HIGH DISH

4 big (ripe & firm) peaches (aadus)
6 tbsp sugar
8-10 tbsp water

SAUCE
1 tbsp vanilla custard powder dissolved in ¼ cup water

DECORATION
a few grapes
a few almonds - split into 2 halves

1. Wash peaches well. Divide into two halves by running a knife all around at the centre. Pull the two parts apart to divide into two equal halves. Remove the seed carefully.
2. Place them in a flat dish. Sprinkle sugar with a tbsp on all the peaches.
3. Pour a tbsp of water on each piece.
4. Micro high for 4 minutes or till the peaches turn very soft, depending upon the ripeness of the fruit.
5. Remove the stewed peaches in a clean serving dish, leaving behind the sugar syrup. Arrange properly and keep aside.
6. Dissolve custard powder in ¼ cup water and add to the sugar syrup.
7. Micro high the sugar syrup for 1 minute, stirring once after 80 seconds or when it starts to boil, to prevent lumps from forming.
8. Pour the ready sauce over the arranged peaches in the dish. Decorate the peaches by placing a fresh cherry or a grape in the centre of each piece and a piece of almond with it.

Chocolate Walnut Cake

Bake a perfect cake in just 4 minutes!

Picture on page 1 Serves 4-5

5-6" ROUND, 4-5" HIGH DISH

2 eggs
¾ cup powdered sugar (sugar has to be powdered, otherwise it burns)
2 tbsp cocoa powder
½ cup maida (flour)
1 tsp baking powder
¼ cup milk
½ cup oil
½ tsp vanilla essence
4 tbsp chopped walnuts
some chocolate sauce (ready made)

1. Beat eggs and sugar till the eggs turn fluffy and the mixture becomes more than double in volume. Add essence.
2. Sift flour with baking powder and cocoa. Keep aside.
3. Mix 1 tsp of maida with 2 tbsp chopped walnuts and keep aside.
4. Add oil to beaten egg-sugar mixture in the pan. Mix well.
5. Fold in flour gradually till all the flour is used. Add walnuts mix with maida. Add milk to get a slightly thinner than a soft dropping consistency. Beat gently, at low speed if you are using an electric egg beater.
6. Grease a deep bowl. Pour the batter in it. Micro high uncovered for 4 minutes. Do not microwave for a longer time even if the surface of the cake does not feel firm and it appears wet after 4 minutes.
7. Let it stand for 4-5 minutes.
8. Let it cool 5-10 minutes before removing from baking dish.
9. Swirl chocolate sauce over it and sprinkle some walnuts. Serve after a little while.

Lychee Pearls in Shahi Kheer

Serves 4-5

10 fresh or canned lychees
10 almonds - blanched
3-4 sheets of varak (silver sheets)

SHAHI KHEER
3 cups milk (½ kg)
1 cup boiled rice
¼ tin condensed milk
1 cup grated paneer
10 almonds - cut into thin long piece
1 tbsp kishmish - soaked
a few drops kewra essence
2 illaichi - powdered

DECORATION
¼ tsp kesar - soaked in 1 tsp warm water
a few rose (desi gulab) petals

1. Micro high 3 cups milk and rice for 8 minutes or till it boils.
2. Reduce power to 60% and microwave for 20 minutes, stirring once in between.
3. Remove from microwave. Mash rice well.
4. Add all other ingredients of the shahi kheer. Transfer to a shallow serving dish. Keep to chill in the fridge.
5. Remove seeds of lychees carefully. Insert an almond in each.
6. Place 3-4 lychees on a varak at intervals. Pick up the varak alng with the lychees carefully such as to coat 3-4 lychees with one sheet of varak. Keep aside covered till serving time in the fridge.
7. At serving time, arrange the lychees on the kheer. Dot with some kesar and sprinkle 1-2 rose petals.

Vanilla Cake

Serves 4-6

5-6" ROUND, 4-5 " DEEP DISH (FILL ONLY HALF)

2 eggs
½ cup powdered sugar (sugar has to be powdered, otherwise it burns)
1 tsp vanilla essence, 2 drops yellow colour, ¼ cup milk
½ cup maida (flour), 1 level tsp baking powder, ½ cup oil

1. Sieve flour and baking powder together.
2. Beat sugar and eggs very well together (with an electric egg beater).
3. Add oil gradually beating mixture lightly. Add milk and colour.
4. Fold in flour a little at a time, with a wooden spoon, till all the flour is used up. Pour into a greased dish and Micro high uncovered for 4 minutes. The cake will appear wet. Do not over bake. Let it stand 4-5 minutes. Let it cool for 5-10 minutes before removing from dish.

Tandoori Fish: Recipe on page 79

BEST SELLERS BY *Nita Mehta*

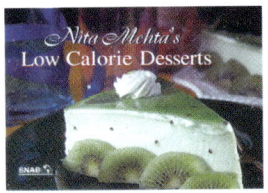

- Low Calorie Desserts
- CONTINENTAL-NV
- Punjabi Cooking
- Taste of KASHMIR
- ITALIAN-NV
- OVEN Recipes-NV
- Taste of RAJASTHAN
- The Best of MUTTON
- MORE CHICKEN
- Great Ideas - Cooking Tips
- LOSE WEIGHT
- SANDWICHES

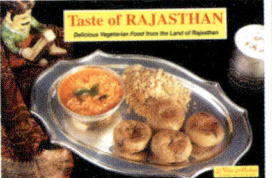

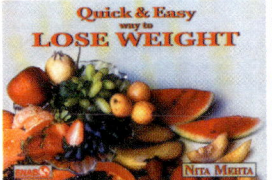